CLASSICAL FAVORITES

FOR HARMONICA

ARRANGED BY

BOBBY JOE HOLMAN

TIP BOX
To play all the music in this book,
try Bobby Joe's "BAG-OF-HARPS."
To purchase, contact:
Musicians Boulevard
2511 E. Thousand Oaks Blvd.
Thousand Oaks, CA 91362
Tel (805) 494-4683
Fax (805) 497-1386

ISBN 978-0-634-01673-8

HAL•LEONARD®
CORPORATION

7777 W. BLUEMOUND RD. P.O. BOX 13819 MILWAUKEE, WI 53213

Visit Hal Leonard Online at
www.halleonard.com

CLASSICAL FAVORITES

FOR HARMONICA

CONTENTS

How to Use the Music in This Book

This book is part of an ongoing series of themed publications covering a wide variety of musical styles. Each one provides a selection of the most popular and requested songs arranged for both the diatonic and chromatic harmonicas.

To understand the techniques required to play the songs presented, it is recommended that you thoroughly study both of my harmonica instruction books: The Hal Leonard Complete Harmonica Method—Book One—The Diatonic Harmonica, and The Hal Leonard Complete Harmonica Method—Book Two—The Chromatic Harmonica

Understanding this system will enable you to fully enjoy the musical treasures found within.

Heart to Harp,

Bobby Joe Holman

Understanding Harmonica Tablature for the Diatonic Harmonica

Before attempting to play the songs in this book, make sure you understand each harmonica tablature symbol, shown below. Understanding these symbols and reading the information on each song will enable you to learn and play these songs more easily and quickly.

To understand how to bend notes and which notes can be bent on a diatonic harmonica, refer to The Hal Leonard Complete Harmonica Method–Book One–The Diatonica Harmonica, Chapter 1. The diatonic harmonica, due to design limitations, requires this many symbols.

Blow	**Draw**
Half-step bend (example: blow bend an E note down to an E♭/D♯)	**Half-step bend** (example: draw bend an E note down to an E♭/D♯)
Whole-step bend (example: blow bend a G note down to an F)	**Whole-step bend** (example: draw bend a G note down to an F)
One and a half-step bend (example: blow bend a C note down to an A)	**One and a half-step bend** (example: draw bend a C note down to an A)

1 – 10   Hole numbers on a diatonic harmonica

A7   Chord symbols for musical accompaniment

E♭ to C   Change from one diatonic harmonica to another in a different key

Two-Part Invention in C Major

By Johann Sebastian Bach

Key: C
Harmonica: C

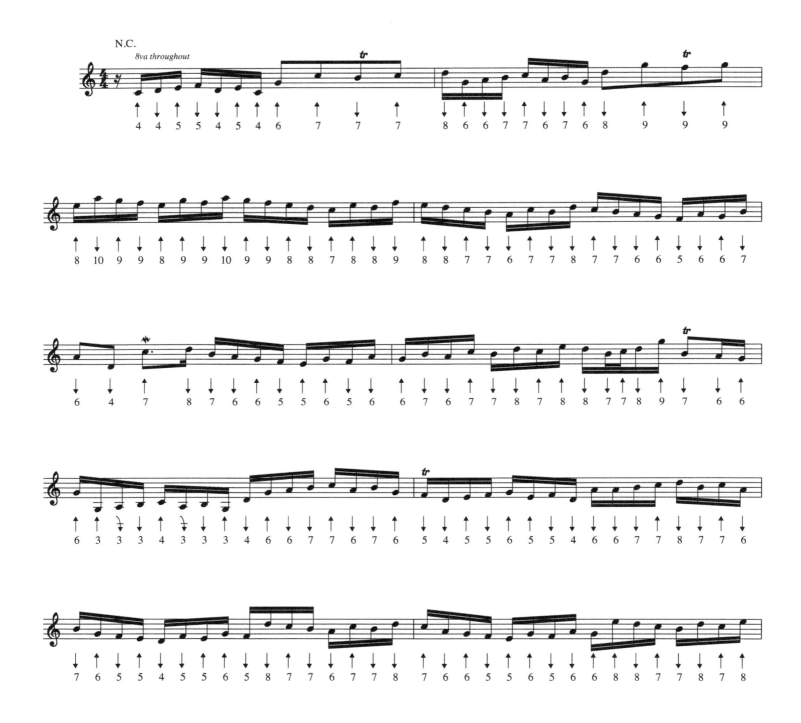

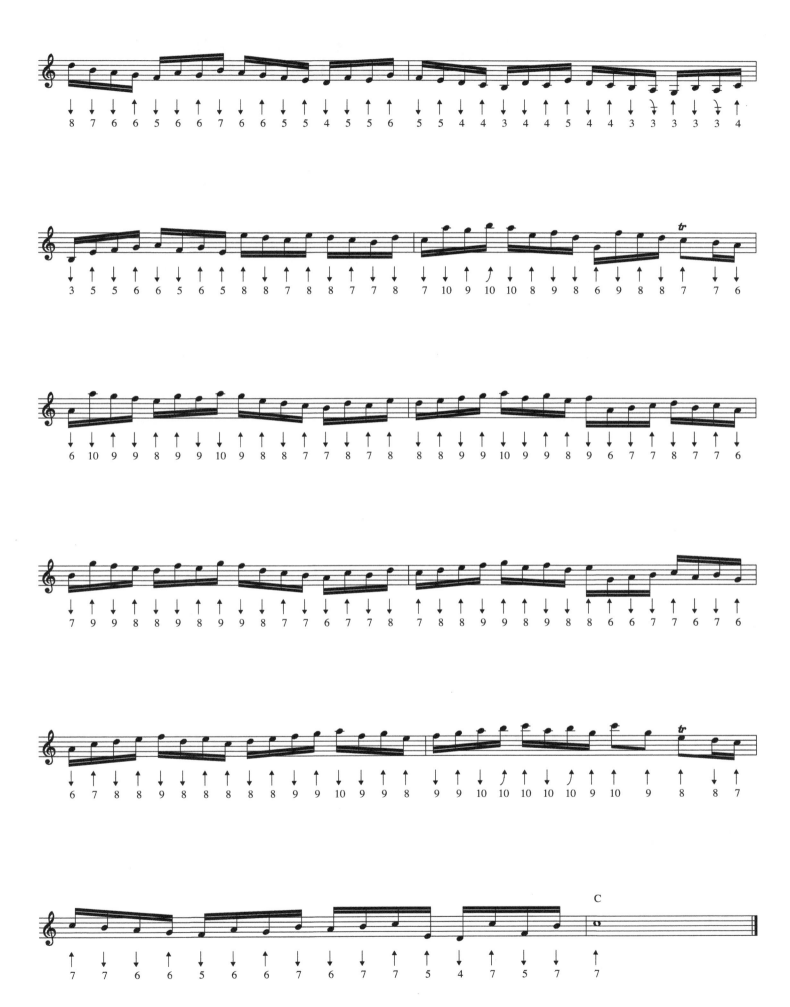

Piano Sonata No. 14 in C♯ Minor ("Moonlight")
First Movement Theme
By Ludwig van Beethoven

Key: E
Harmonica: E

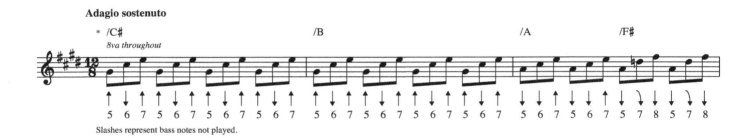

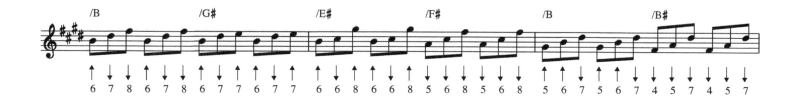

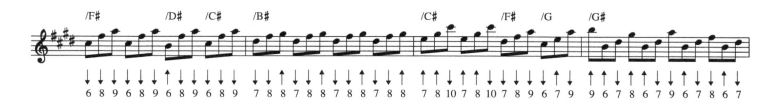

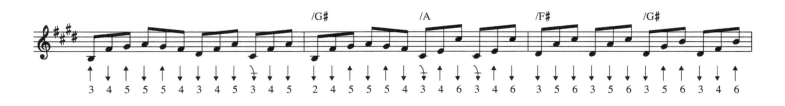

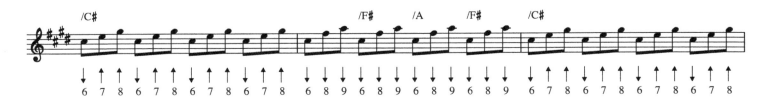

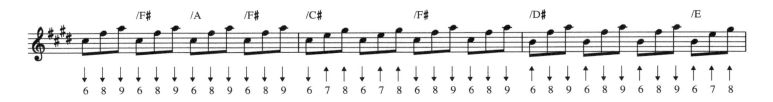

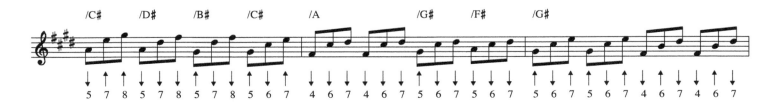

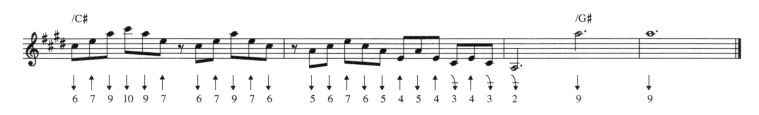

Symphony No. 5 in C Minor
Op. 67
First Movement Theme
By Ludwig van Beethoven

Key: Eb
Harmonicas: Eb, C

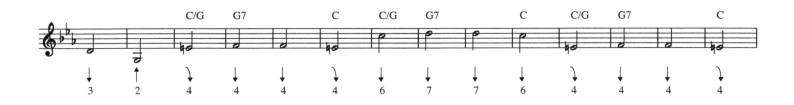

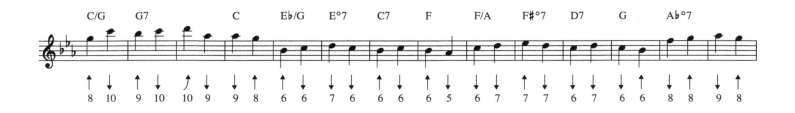

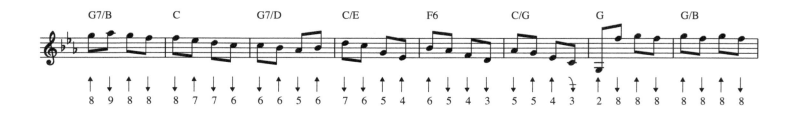

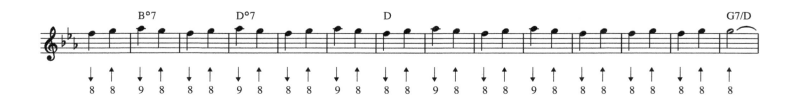

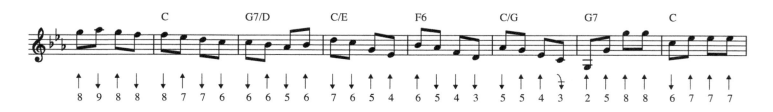

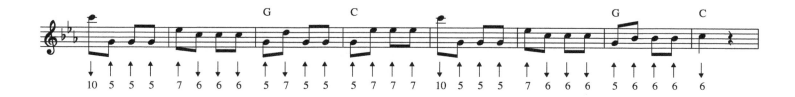

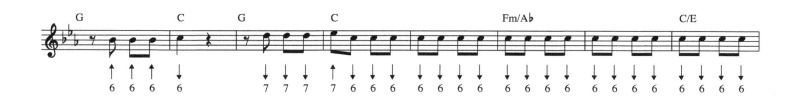

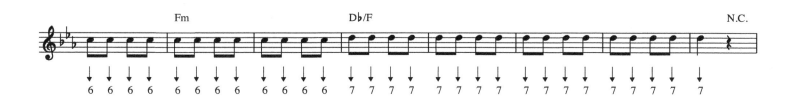

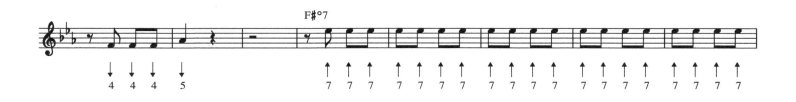

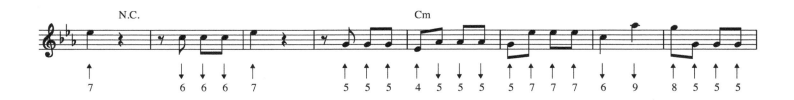

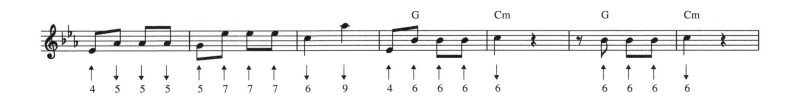

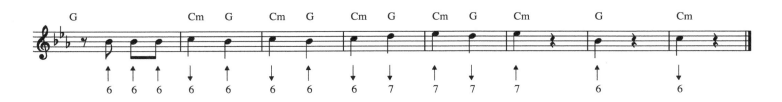

Symphony No. 6 in F Major ("Pastoral")
Op. 68
Third Movement Theme
By Ludwig van Beethoven

Key: F
Harmonica: F

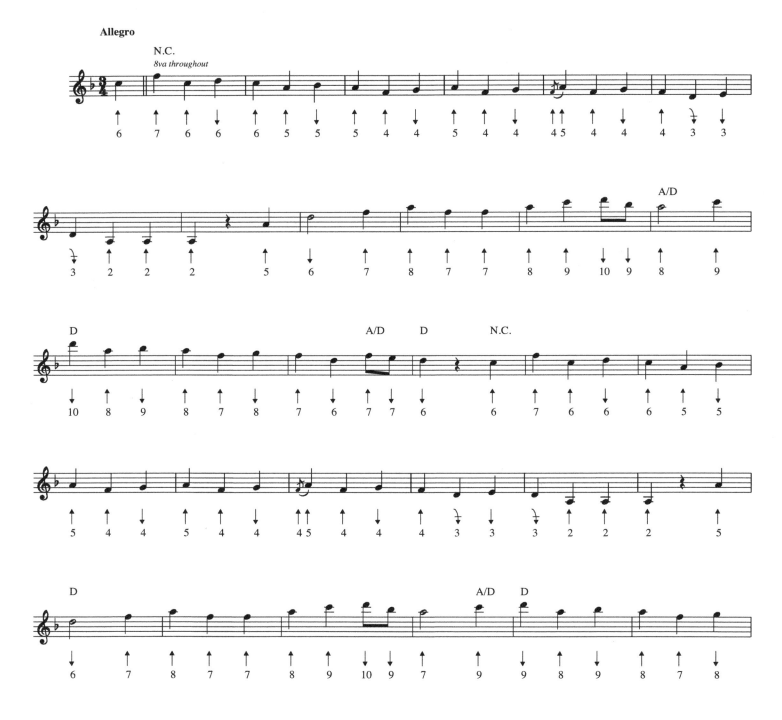

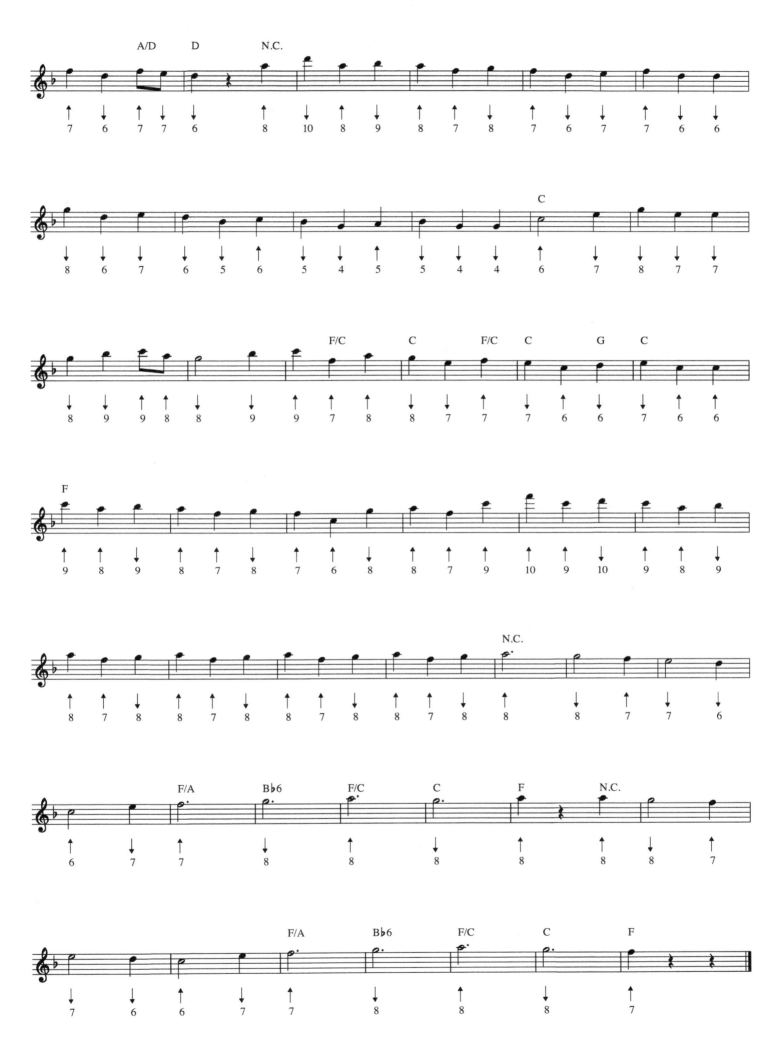

Symphony No. 9 in D Minor
Op. 125
Second Movement Theme

By Ludwig van Beethoven

Key: D minor
Harmonica: C, A

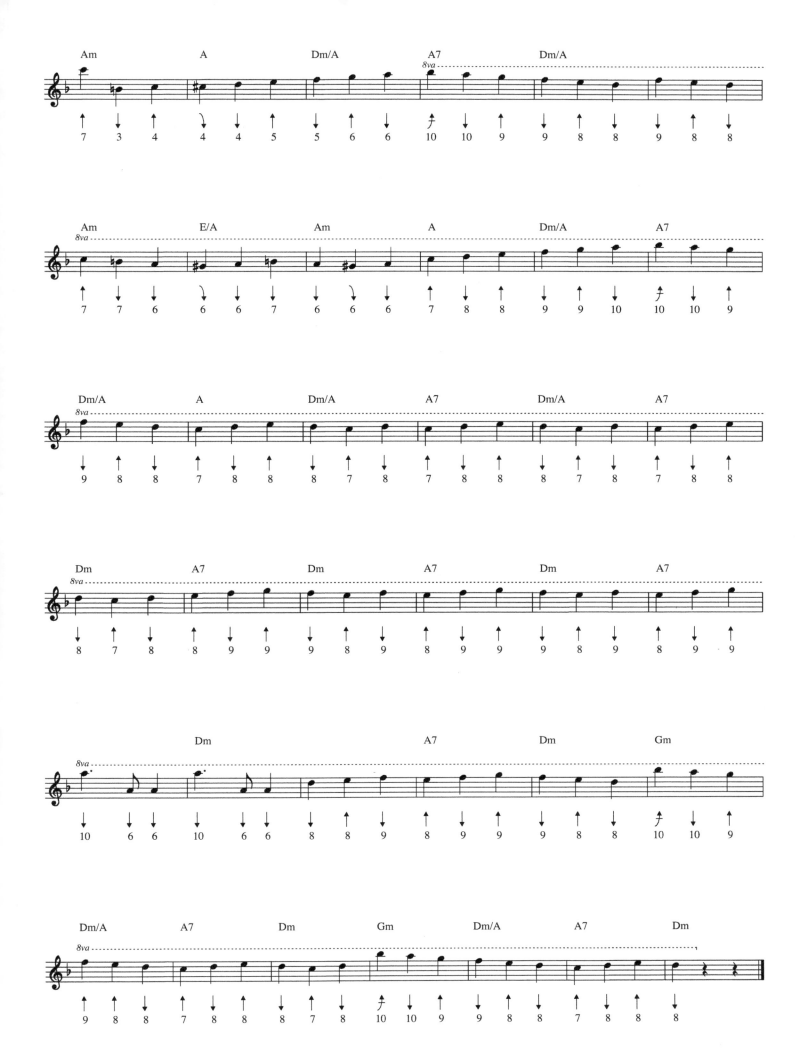

Waltz in C♯ Minor
Op. 64, No. 2
By Fryderyk Chopin

Key: C♯ minor
Harmonica: E

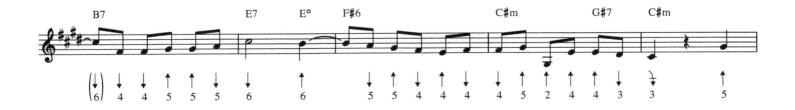

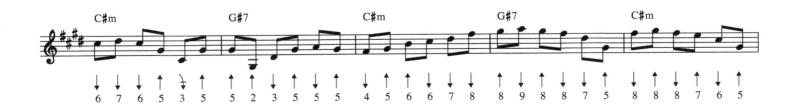

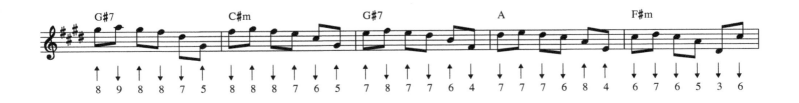

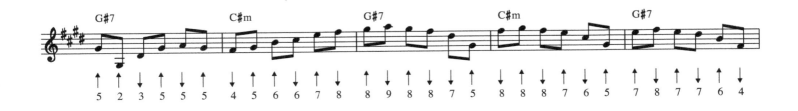

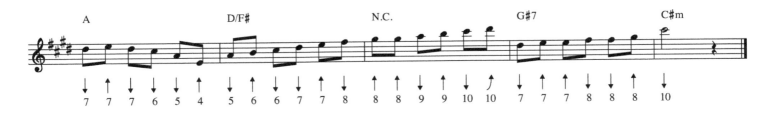

Gypsy Rondo
Piano Trio No. 1
By Franz Joseph Haydn

Key: G
Harmonica: G, B♭

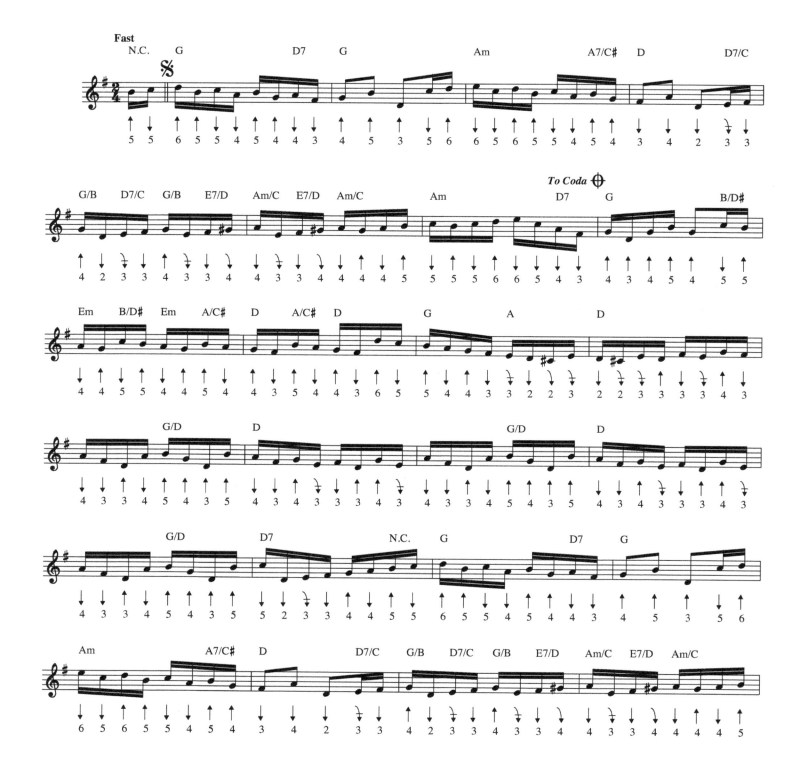

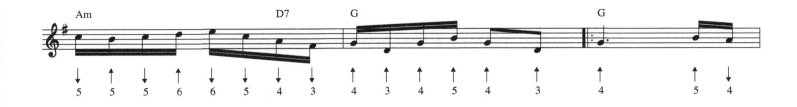

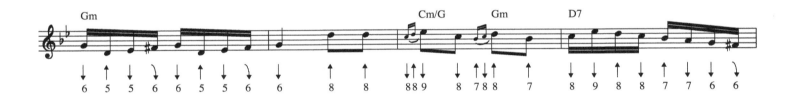

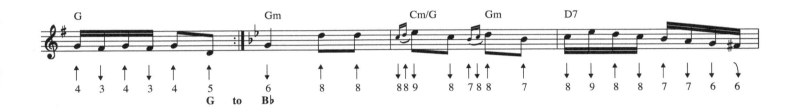

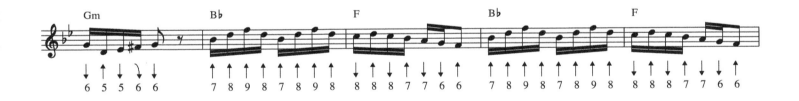

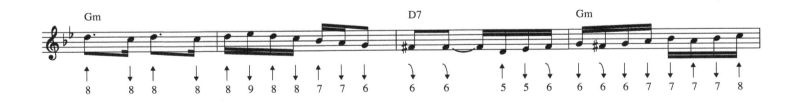

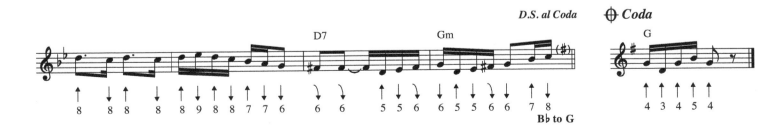

Lascia Ch'io Pianga
from RINALDO

By George Frideric Handel

Key: F
Harmonica: F

Surprise Symphony
Second Movement Theme
By Franz Joseph Haydn

Key: F
Harmonica: F

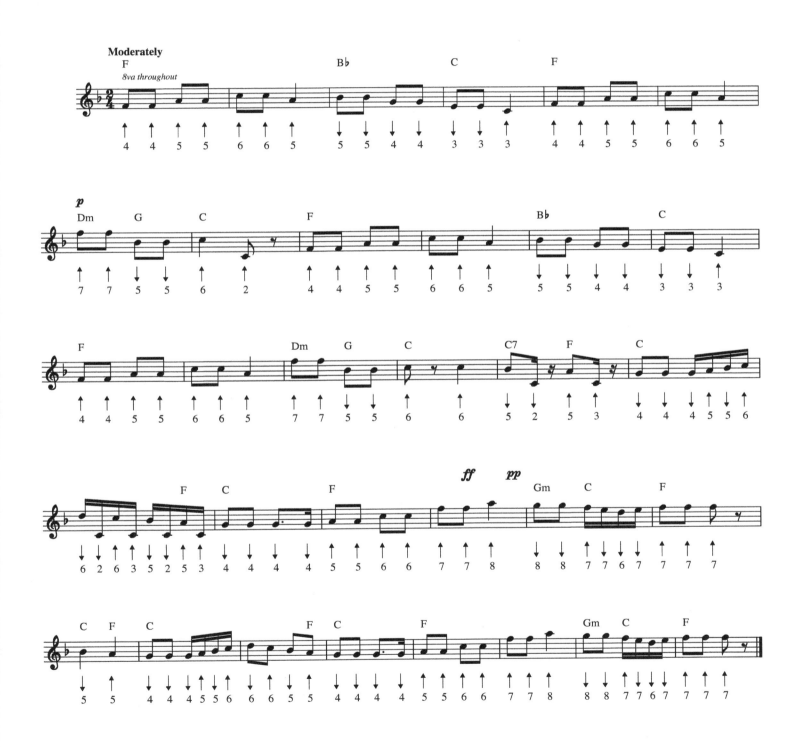

Minuet
from DON GIOVANNI
By Wolfgang Amadeus Mozart

Key: F
Harmonica: F

The Swan (Le Cygne)
from CARNIVAL OF THE ANIMALS
By Camille Saint-Saëns

Key: G
Harmonica: G

Minuet in G Major, K. 1

By Wolfgang Amadeus Mozart

Key: G
Harmonica: G

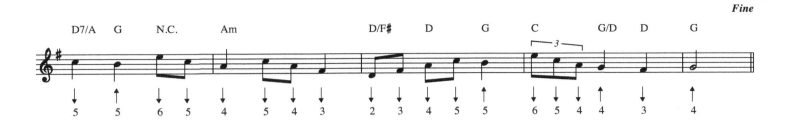

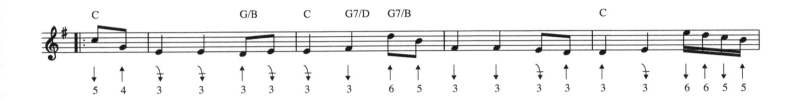

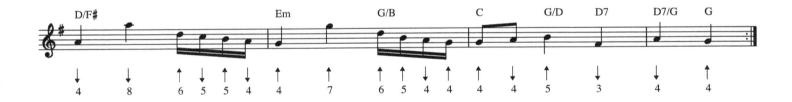

D.S. al Fine

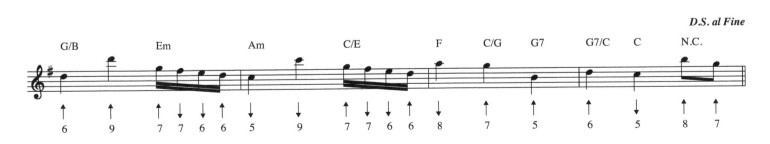

Prelude in G Minor
Op. 23, No. 5
By Serge Rachmaninoff

Key: G minor
Harmonica: Bb

A la Marcia

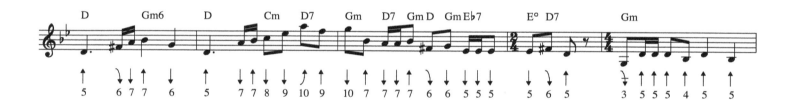

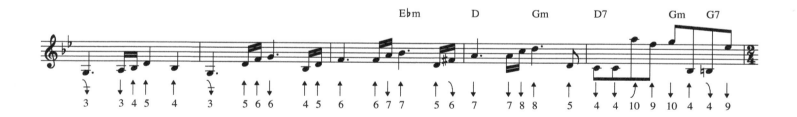

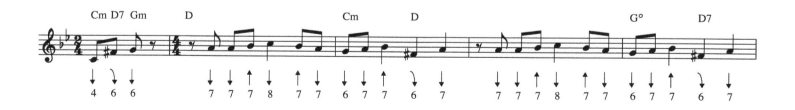

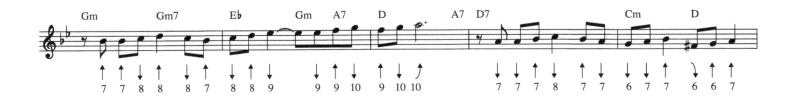

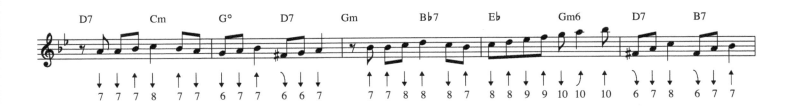

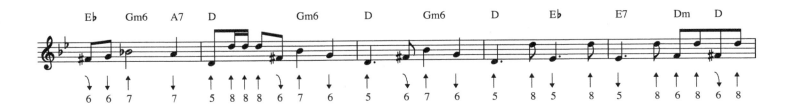

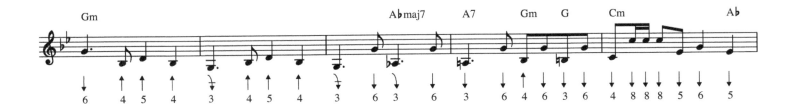

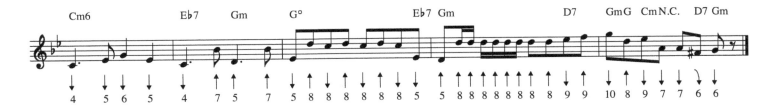

Waltz of the Flowers
from THE NUTCRACKER
By Pyotr Il'yich Tchaikovsky

Key: D
Harmonica: D

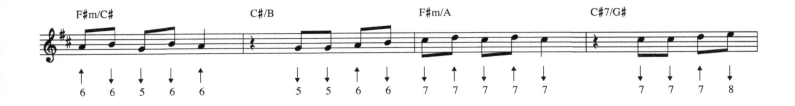

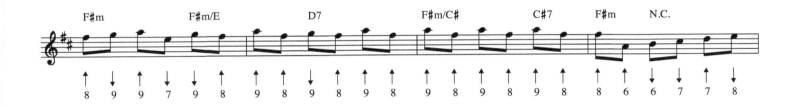

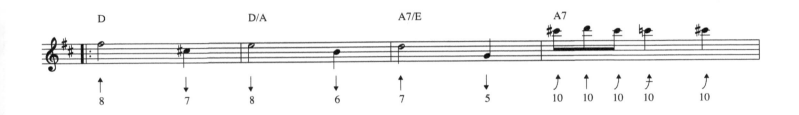

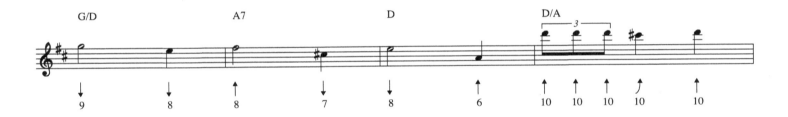

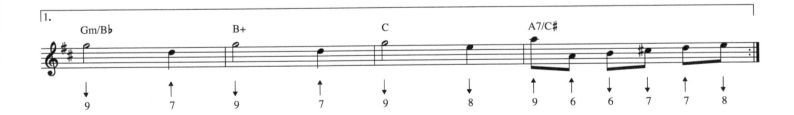

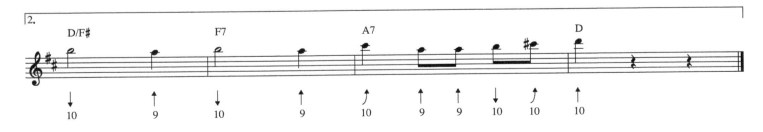

Theme from Swan Lake

By Pyotr Il'yich Tchaikovsky

Key: A minor
Harmonica: C

By the Beautiful Blue Danube

By Johann Strauss, Jr.

Key: D
Harmonica: D, A

Clair de Lune
from SUITE BERGAMESQUE
By Claude Debussy

Key: C
Harmonica: C

Understanding Harmonica Tablature for the Chromatic Harmonica

Before attempting to play the songs in this section, the same approach is required to play these songs as in the diatonic section of this book. Make sure you understand each harmonica tablature symbol shown below to expedite the learning process.

Unlike the diatonic harmonica, the chromatic harmonica was designed to play every note in a two-octave scale (Hohner Chrometta #250), two and a half-octave scale (Hohner Chromatica #260), three-octave scale (Hohner Super Chromatica #270 or Chrometta #255) or four-octave scale (Hohner Super 64 #280). There are no bent notes required or changing of keys when playing this music on a chromatic harmonica.

To understand how to play this music on the chromatic harmonica, you should refer to The Hal Leonard Complete Harmonica Method – Book Two – The Chromatic Harmonica.

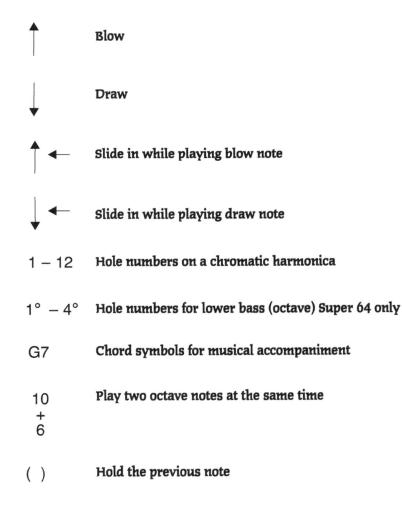

↑	Blow
↓	Draw
↑ ←	Slide in while playing blow note
↓ ←	Slide in while playing draw note
1 – 12	Hole numbers on a chromatic harmonica
1° – 4°	Hole numbers for lower bass (octave) Super 64 only
G7	Chord symbols for musical accompaniment
10 + 6	Play two octave notes at the same time
( )	Hold the previous note

Two-Part Invention in C Major

By Johann Sebastian Bach

Key: C
Harmonica: Hohner Super 64 only

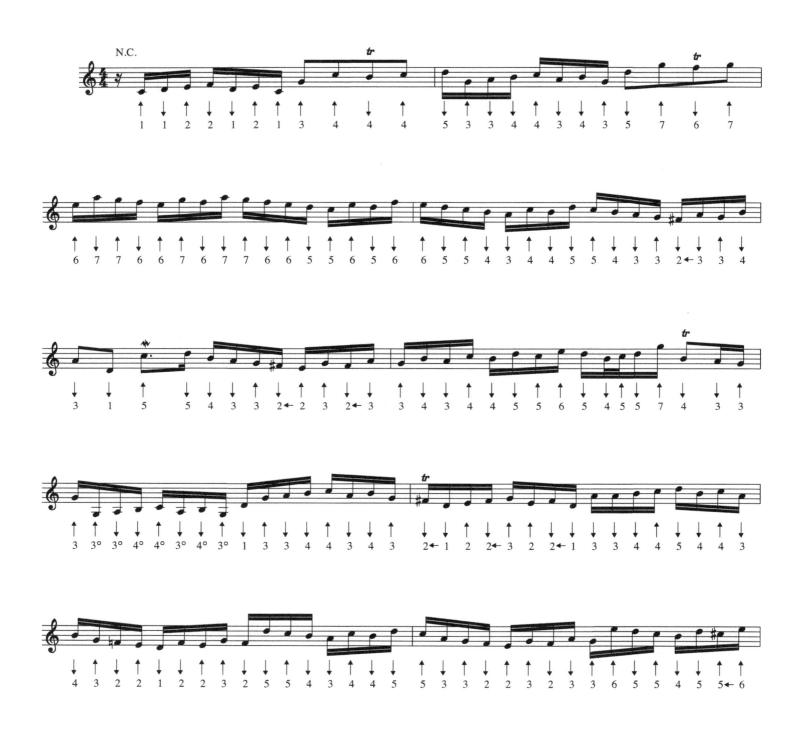

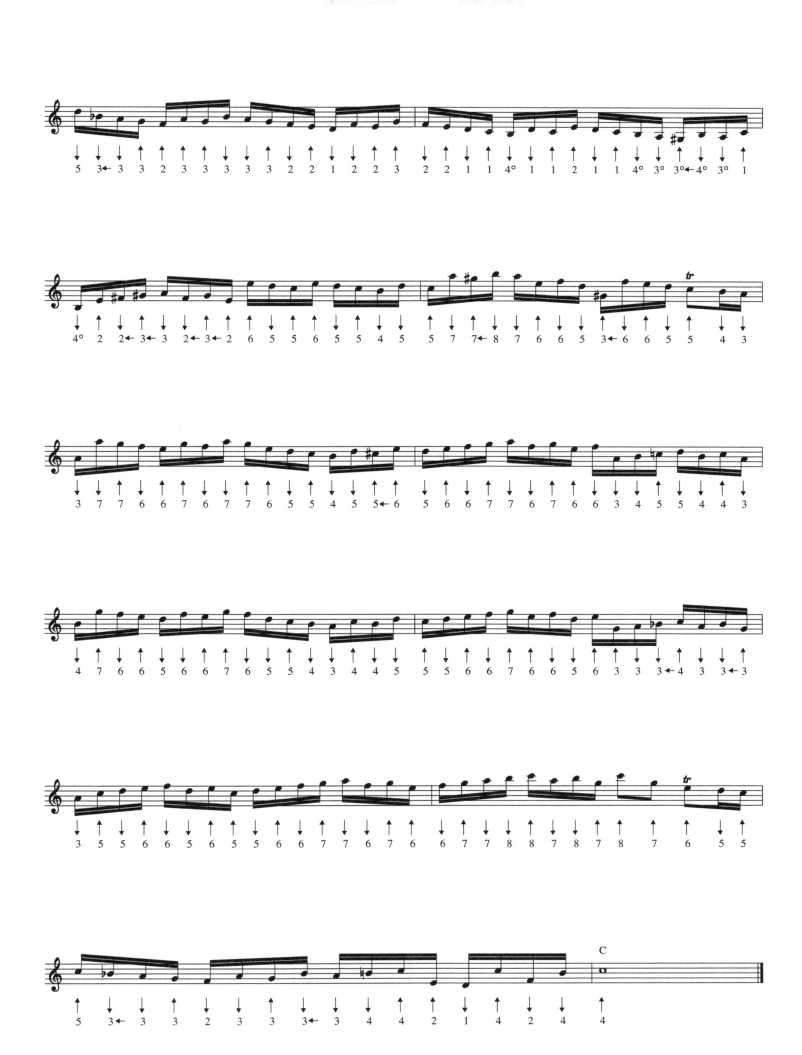

Piano Sonata No. 14 in C♯ Minor ("Moonlight")
First Movement Theme
By Ludwig van Beethoven

Key: E
Harmonica: Hohner Super 64 only

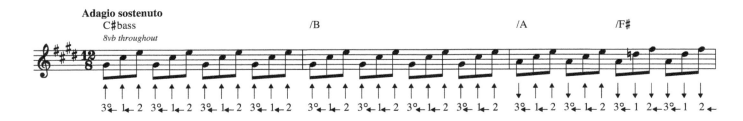

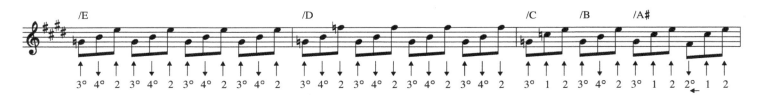

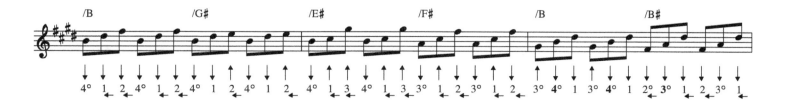

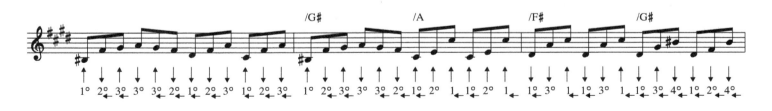

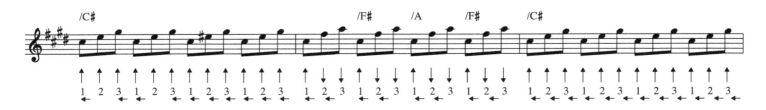

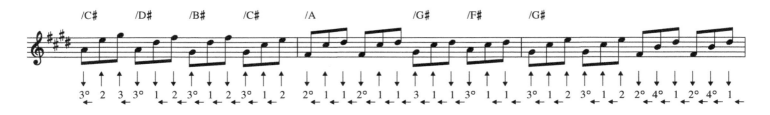

Symphony No. 5 in C Minor
Op. 67
First Movement Theme

By Ludwig van Beethoven

Key: E♭
Harmonica: Hohner Super 64 only

Allegro con brio

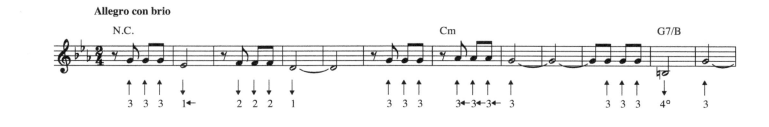

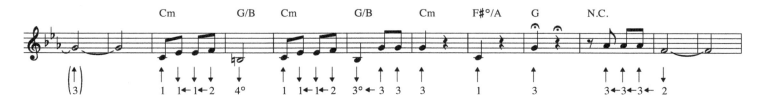

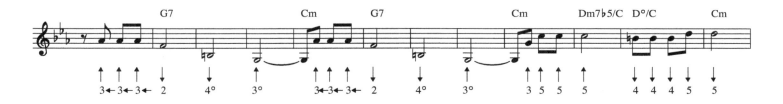

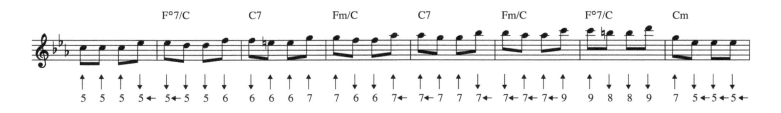

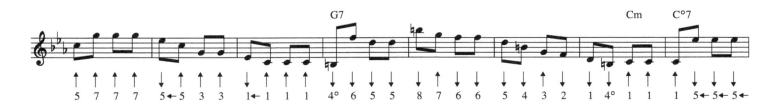

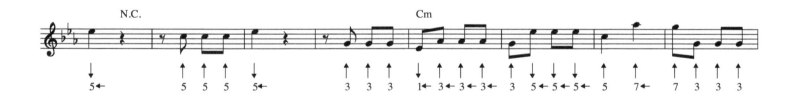

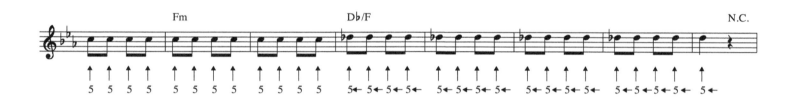

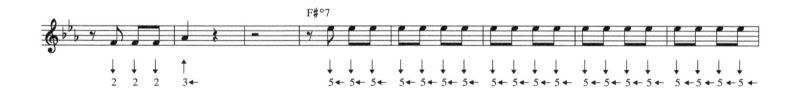

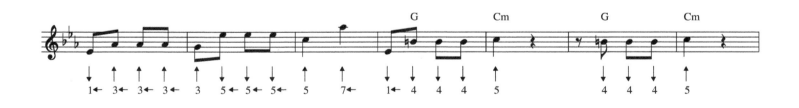

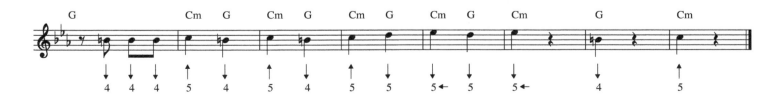

Symphony No. 6 in F Major ("Pastoral")
Third Movement Theme
By Ludwig van Beethoven

Key: F
Harmonica: Hohner Super 64 only

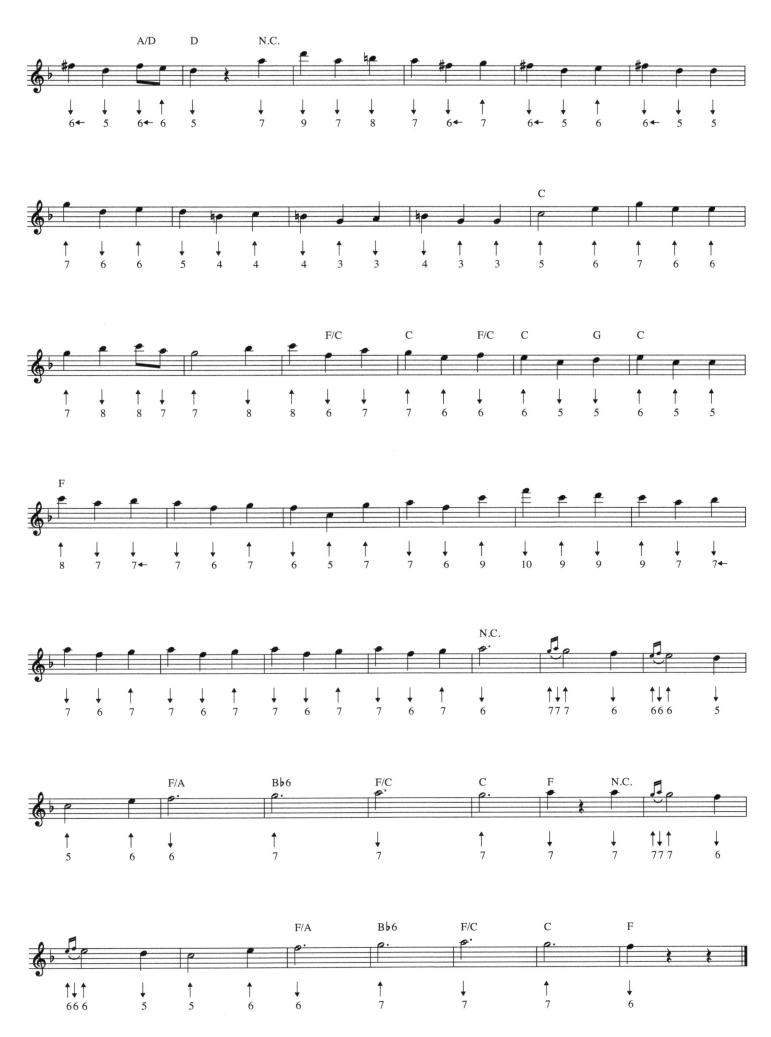

Symphony No. 9 in D Minor
Op. 125
Second Movement Theme

By Ludwig van Beethoven

Key: D minor
Harmonica: Hohner Super 64 only

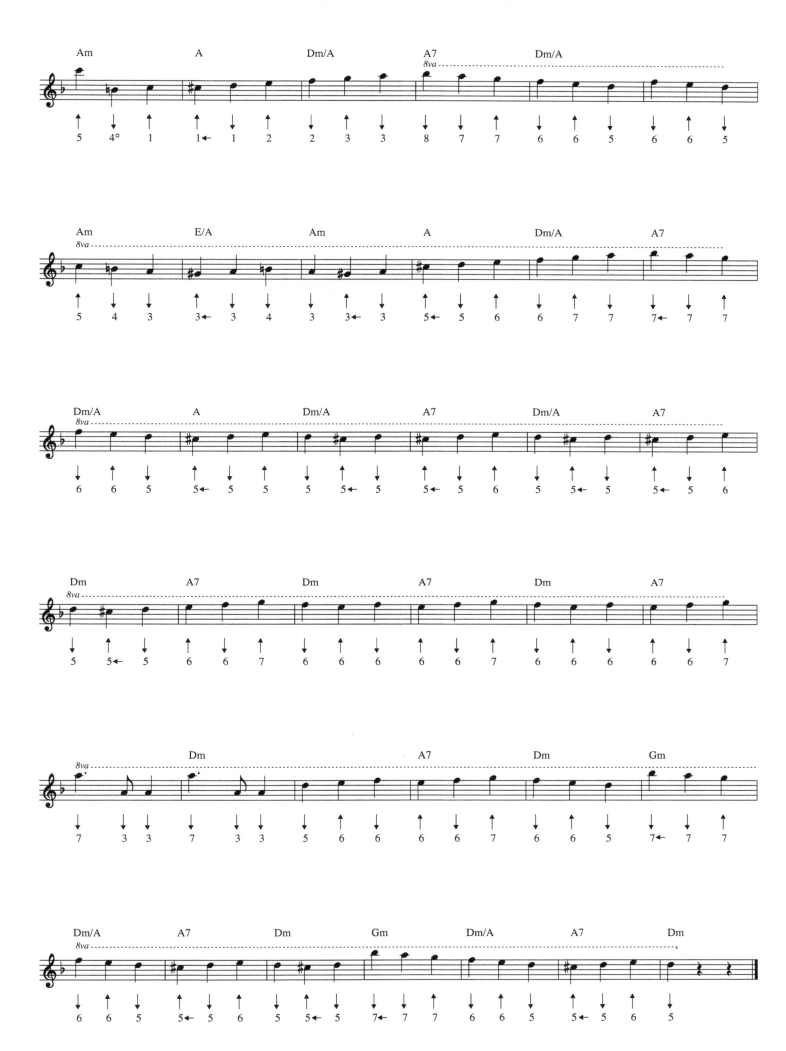

Waltz in C♯ Minor
Op. 64, No. 2
By Fryderyk Chopin

Key: C♯ minor
Harmonica: Hohner Super 64 only

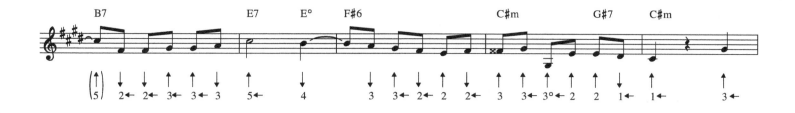

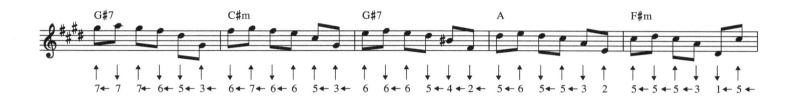

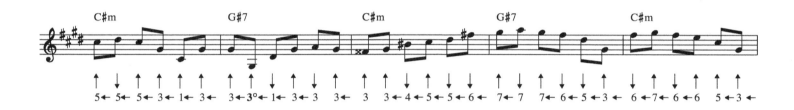

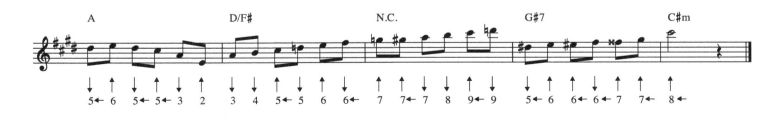

47

Surprise Symphony
Second Movement Theme
By Franz Joseph Haydn

Key: F
Harmonica: All chromatic harmonicas

Minuet
from DON GIOVANNI
By Wolfgang Amadeus Mozart

Key: F
Harmonica: All chromatic harmonicas

Gypsy Rondo
Piano Trio No. 1
By Franz Joseph Haydn

Key: G
Harmonica: Hohner Super 64 only

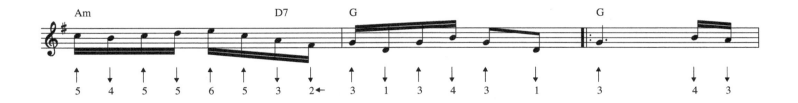

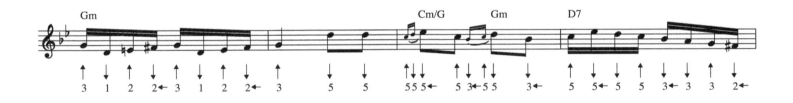

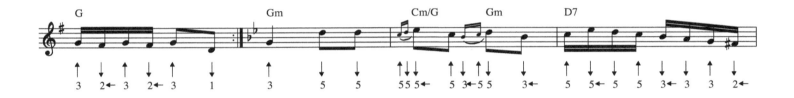

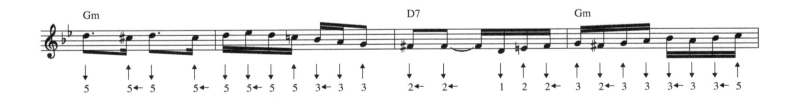

D.S. al Coda ⊕ *Coda*

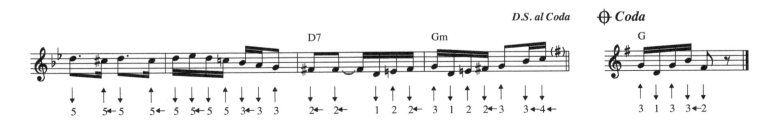

Minuet in G Major, K. 1

By Wolfgang Amadeus Mozart

Key: G
Harmonica: All chromatic harmonicas

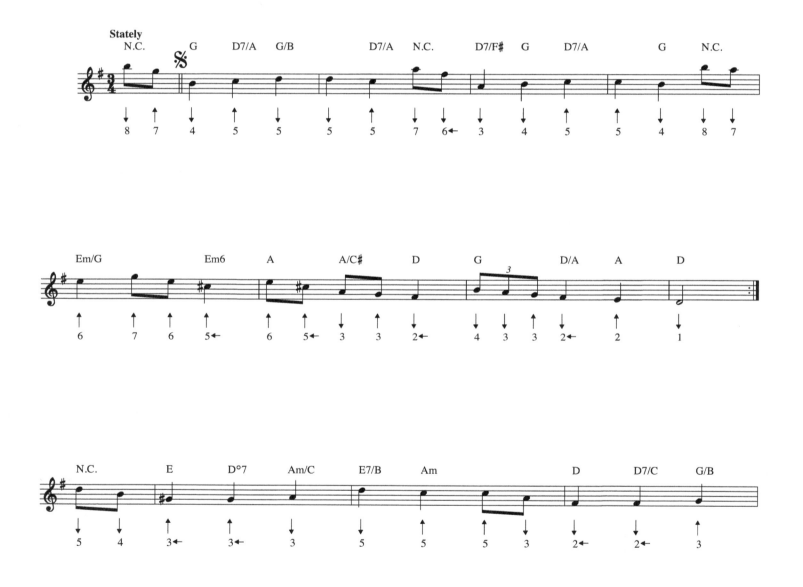

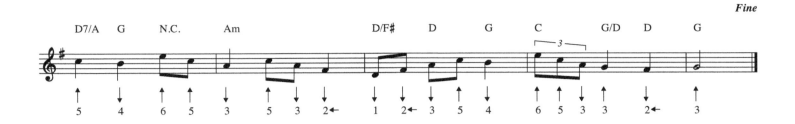

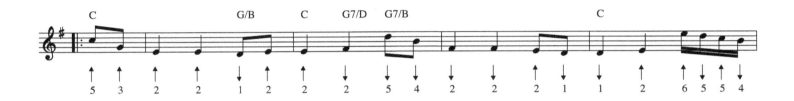

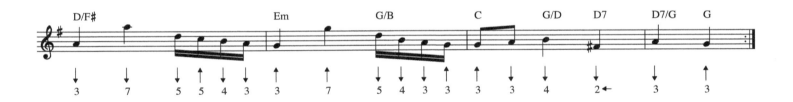

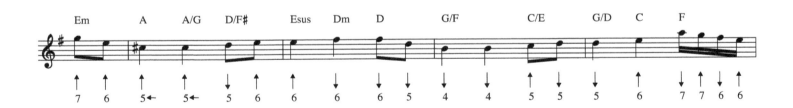

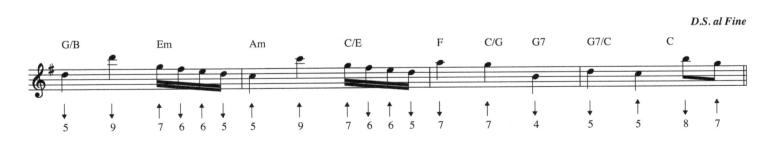

Prelude in G Minor
Op. 23, No. 5
By Serge Rachmaninoff

Key: G minor
Harmonica: Hohner Super 64 only

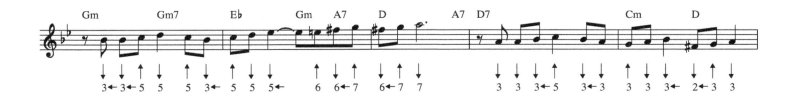

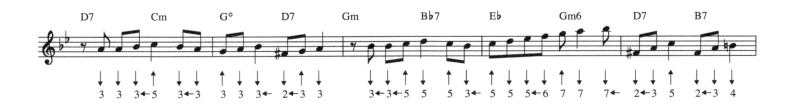

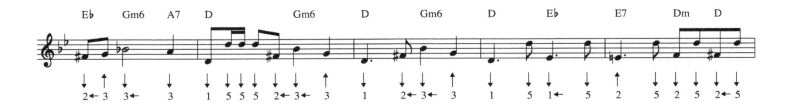

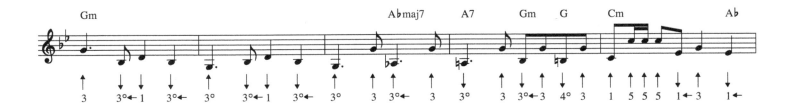

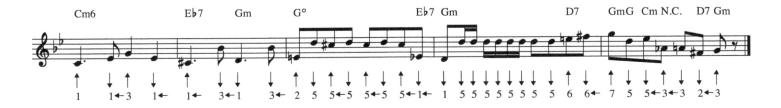

The Flight of the Bumblebee

By Nicolai Rimsky-Korsakov

Key: A minor
Harmonica: Hohner Super 64 only

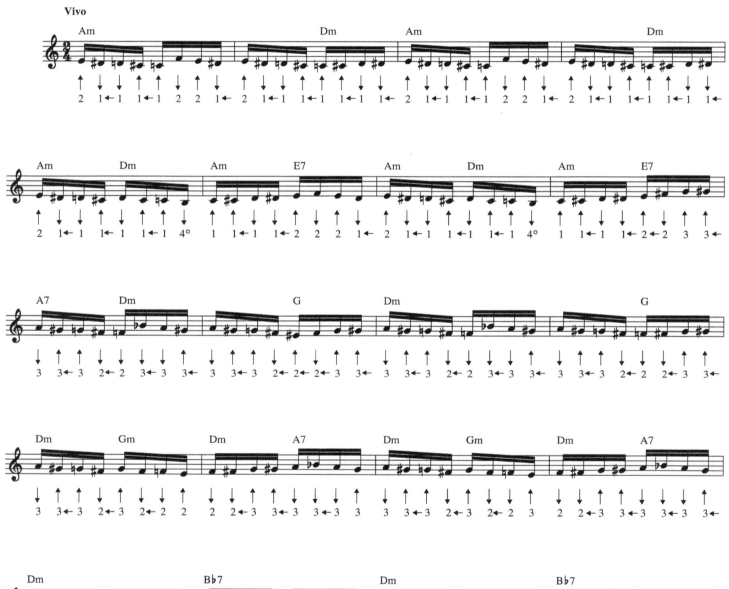

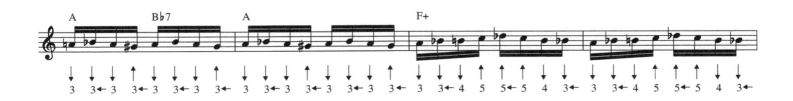

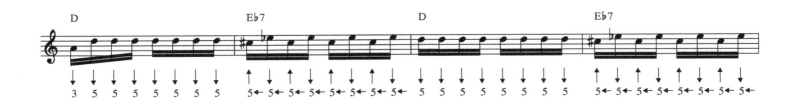

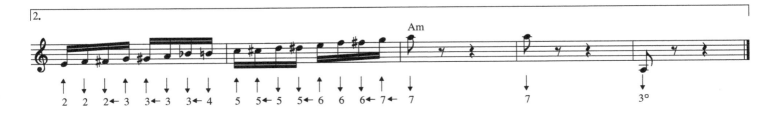

Waltz of the Flowers
from THE NUTCRACKER

By Pyotr Il'yich Tchaikovsky

Key: D
Harmonica: Hohner Super 64 only

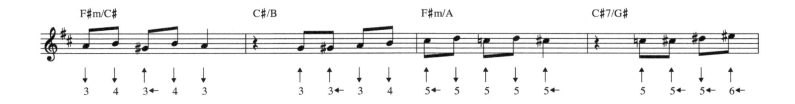

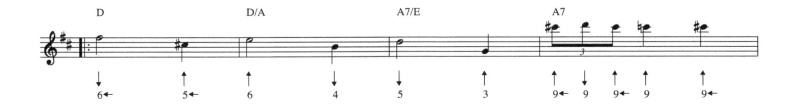

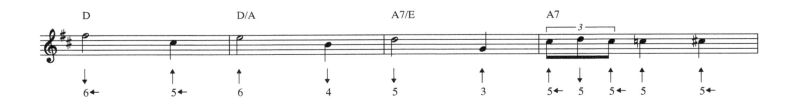

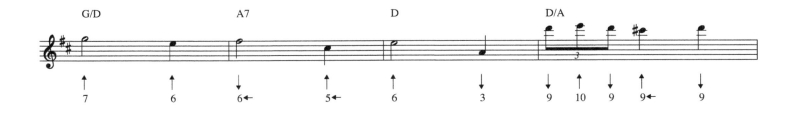

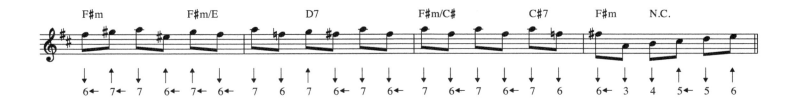

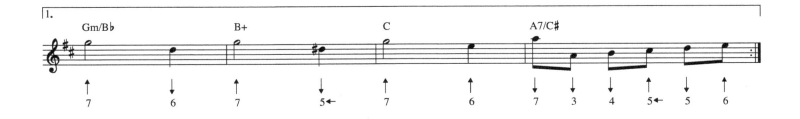

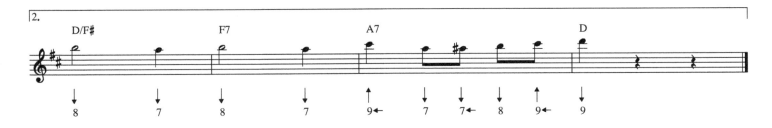

Theme from Swan Lake

By Pyotr Il'yich Tchaikovsky

Key: A minor
Harmonica: All chromatic harmonicas

The Swan (Le Cygne)
from CARNIVAL OF THE ANIMALS
By Camille Saint-Saëns

Key: G
Harmonica: All chromatic harmonicas

By the Beautiful Blue Danube

By Johann Strauss, Jr.

Key: D
Harmonica: Hohner Super 64 only

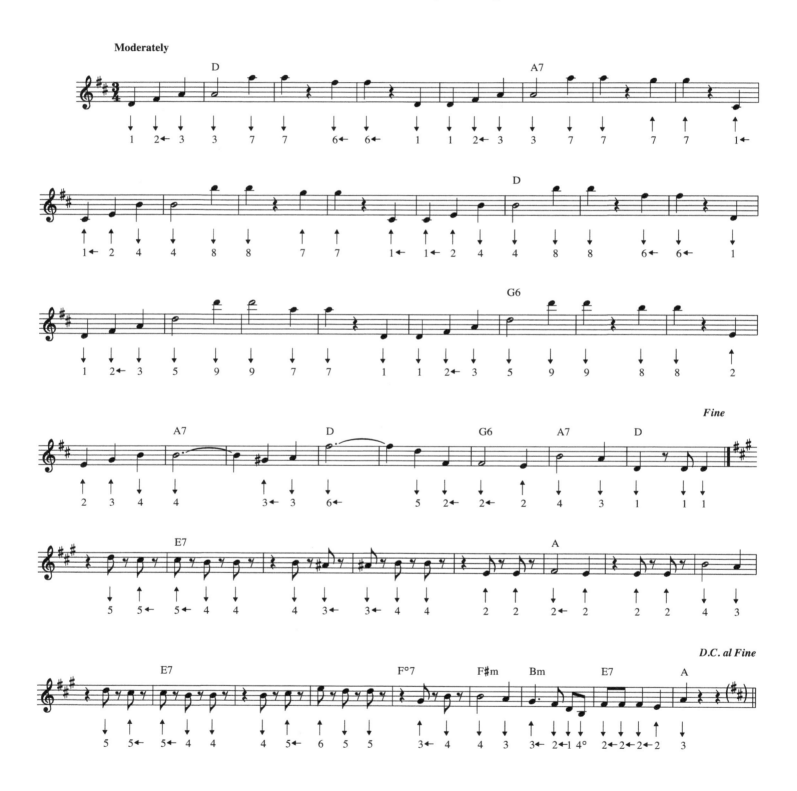

Clair de Lune
from SUITE BERGAMESQUE
By Claude Debussy

Key: C
Harmonica: Hohner Super 64 only

THE HAL LEONARD HARMONICA METHOD AND SONGBOOKS

THE METHOD

THE HAL LEONARD COMPLETE HARMONICA METHOD — CHROMATIC HARMONICA

by Bobby Joe Holman

The only harmonica method to present the chromatic harmonica in 14 scales and modes in all 12 keys! This book will take beginners from the basics on through to the most advanced techniques available for the contemporary harmonica player. Each section contains appropriate songs and exercises that enable the player to quickly learn the various concepts presented. Every aspect of this versatile musical instrument is explored and explained in easy-to-understand detail with illustrations. The musical styles covered include traditional, blues, pop and rock.

00841286 Book/Online Audio............................. $12.99

THE HAL LEONARD COMPLETE HARMONICA METHOD — DIATONIC HARMONICA

by Bobby Joe Holman

The only harmonica method specific to the diatonic harmonica, covering all six positions. This book/audio pack contains over 20 songs and musical examples that take beginners from the basics on through to the most advanced techniques available for the contemporary harmonica player. Each section contains appropriate songs and exercises (which are demonstrated through the online video) that enable the player to quickly learn the various concepts presented. Every aspect of this versatile musical instrument is explored and explained in easy-to-understand detail with illustrations. The musical styles covered include traditional, blues, pop and rock.

00841285 Book/Online Audio............................. $12.99

THE SONGBOOKS

The Hal Leonard Harmonica Songbook series offers a wide variety of music especially tailored to the two-volume Hal Leonard Harmonica Method, but can be played by all harmonica players, diatonic and chromatic alike. All books include study and performance notes, and a guide to harmonica tablature. From classical themes to Christmas music, rock and roll to Broadway, there's something for everyone!

BROADWAY SONGS FOR HARMONICA `INCLUDES TAB`

arranged by Bobby Joe Holman

19 show-stopping Broadway tunes for the harmonica. Songs include: Ain't Misbehavin' • Bali Ha'i • Camelot • Climb Ev'ry Mountain • Do-Re-Mi • Edelweiss • Give My Regards to Broadway • Hello, Dolly! • I've Grown Accustomed to Her Face • The Impossible Dream (The Quest) • Memory • Oklahoma • People • and more.

00820009..$9.95

CLASSICAL FAVORITES FOR HARMONICA `INCLUDES TAB`

arranged by Bobby Joe Holman

18 famous classical melodies and themes, arranged for diatonic and chromatic players. Includes: By the Beautiful Blue Danube • Clair De Lune • The Flight of the Bumble Bee • Gypsy Rondo • Moonlight Sonata • Surprise Symphony • The Swan (Le Cygne) • Waltz of the Flowers • and more, plus a guide to harmonica tablature.

00820006..$10.99

MOVIE FAVORITES FOR HARMONICA `INCLUDES TAB`

arranged by Bobby Joe Holman

19 songs from the silver screen, arranged for diatonic and chromatic harmonica. Includes: Alfie • Bless the Beasts and Children • Chim Chim Cher-ee • The Entertainer • Georgy Girl • Midnight Cowboy • Moon River • Picnic • Speak Softly, Love • Stormy Weather • Tenderly • Unchained Melody • What a Wonderful World • and more, plus a guide to harmonica tablature.

00820014 ....$9.95

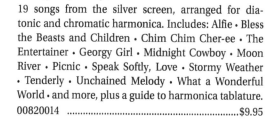

HAL•LEONARD®

Visit Hal Leonard Online at
www.halleonard.com